WRITING STORIES

ANIMAL STORIES

Anita Ganeri

Raintree is an imprint of Capstone Global Library Limited, a company incorporated in England and Wales having its registered office at 7 Pilgrim Street, London, EC4V 6LB – Registered company number: 6695582

To contact Raintree:
Phone: 0845 6044371
Fax: + 44 (0) 1865 312263
Email: myorders@raintreepublishers.co.uk
Outside the UK please telephone +44 1865 312262.

Text © Capstone Global Library Limited 2013
First published in hardback in 2013
The moral rights of the proprietor have been asserted.

Edited by Dan Nunn, Rebecca Rissman, and Sian Smith
Designed by Joanna Hinton-Malivoire
Original illustrations © Capstone Global Library 2013
Picture research by Ruth Blair
Production by Sophia Argyris
Originated by Capstone Global Library Ltd
Printed and bound in China by South China Printing Company Ltd

ISBN 978 1 406 26036 6
17 16 15 14 13
10 9 8 7 6 5 4 3 2 1

British Library Cataloguing in Publication Data
Ganeri, Anita, 1961-
Animal stories. -- (Writing stories) 1. Fiction--Authorship--Juvenile literature. 2. Animals in literature--Juvenile literature. 3. Children's stories.
I. Title II. Series
808.3-dc23

Acknowledgements
We would like to thank the following for permission to reproduce photographs: Alamy pp.5, 7; Getty Images p.16 (Gary S Chapman); Shutterstock background images and design features, pp.4 (© Darrin Henry), 6 (© Abramova Kseniya), 8 (© Mat Hayward), 9 (© Zurijeta), 12 (© Eric Isselée), 14 (© Daniel Krylov), 16 (© Eric Isselée), 18 (© K Chelette), 22 (© Yuri Arcurs), 24 (© Sue McDonald), 26 (© Eric Isselée).

Cover photograph reproduced with permission of Shutterstock (© Eric Isselée).

Every effort has been made to contact copyright holders of material reproduced in this book. Any omissions will be rectified in subsequent printings if notice is given to the publisher.

Some words are shown in bold, **like this**. You can find out what they mean by looking in the glossary.

Contents

Follow this symbol to read an animal story.

What is a story?

A story is a piece of **fiction** writing. It tells the reader about made-up people, places, and events. Anyone can make up a story. You need to choose a **setting**, some **characters**, and a **plot**. Then you can start writing.

There are many different types of stories. You can write mystery stories, silly stories, fairy tales, spooky stories, adventure stories, and so on. This book is about writing animal stories.

Animal stories

An animal story can be about a pet animal or about an animal that lives in the wild. You can base the story on your own pet, an animal that you have read about, or just your imagination!

Black Beauty is a famous book about a horse.

The Tortoise and the Hare is one of a collection of stories, called Aesop's **Fables**.

Some stories use animal **characters** to teach a lesson. In *The Tortoise and the Hare,* a hare makes fun of a tortoise for being slow. The tortoise challenges the hare to a race. Thinking that he will win easily, the hare takes a nap and then the tortoise wins the race.

Getting ideas

Ideas for stories can come from books, the internet or TV, or your imagination. Sometimes, an interesting animal fact can spark off a great story idea. Then you can do more research about the animals you are writing about.

Have you ever had a really good idea, then forgotten it? Keep a notebook and pencil handy for jotting down ideas. Then you will remember them when you come to write your story.

Plot planning

What happens in your story is called the **plot**. It needs a beginning, a middle, and an end. Before you start writing, plan out your plot. You can use a **story mountain**, like the one below, to help you.

Middle
The main action happens. There may be a problem for one of your characters.

Beginning
Set the scene and introduce your main **characters**.

Ending
The problem is solved and the story ends.

Your story starts at one side of the mountain, goes up to the top, then down the other side.

A **timeline** is another way of working out your plot. It can help you to put the events in the right order. Here is a timeline for the animal story in this book.

Boy finds a stray dog on doorstep.

⬇

Boy hides dog in his bedroom.

⬇

Mum hears dog barking.

⬇

Dog chews Dad's best shoes.

⬇

Dad says dog has to go.

⬇

Dog wakes boy up in night.

⬇

Dog warns family about flooded kitchen.

⬇

Dad says dog can stay.

In the beginning

Your story needs a strong beginning. It should grab your readers' attention and make them want to keep reading. It is also where you introduce your main **characters**.

> Can you turn any of these ideas into the beginning of a story?

Animal story ideas

- A stray dog appears on a doorstep.
- A girl gets an elephant as a pet.
- A tiger escapes from a zoo.

An Animal Story

There it was again. It sounded like a whimper and it was coming from outside the front door. Joe went to the door and opened it. There, on the doormat, sat the scruffiest dog Joe had ever seen.

Keep the beginning of your story short so that it grabs your readers' attention straight away.

Setting the scene

The **setting** means the time and place where your story happens. It is like a world that you make up for your story. Writing about what your setting looks, sounds, and even smells like can help you to bring that place to life.

An animal story might happen in a wild place, a zoo or wildlife park, or closer to home.

Joe looked up and down the empty street. Where was the dog's owner? Apart from a few cars, there was no one else about. It was getting dark. Street lights were flickering on.

Joe could smell rain in the air and heard a rumble of thunder. He couldn't leave the small dog outside in the cold and rain.

Imagining that you are in the setting can help you to describe it.

Character building

The **characters** in your story need to be interesting and believable. This is the same for human and animal characters. Think about what they look like, how they behave, and their likes and dislikes. Jot down the details in character fact files.

Character fact file
Character: Joe, a boy
Age: about 8 or 9
Looks like: short, dark hair; wears glasses
Personality: kind; funny; shy
Likes: animals; football; watching cartoons
Dislikes: bananas; homework

Character fact file
Character: dog [no name]
Age: unknown
Looks like: small; brown fur; scruffy
Personality: gentle; mischievous
Likes: food; bones; being stroked
Dislikes: having no home

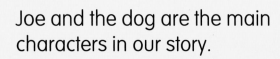

Joe and the dog are the main characters in our story.

The dog looked at Joe. It had scruffy, brown fur and a long tail that wagged and wagged.

It had big, sad, brown eyes. Joe had never had a pet before. He spent a lot of time on his own because he was shy and found it hard to make friends. But Joe loved the sad, scruffy dog as soon as he saw it.

Can you think of a name for the dog that describes what it looks like?

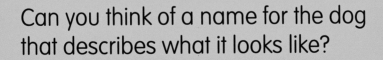

17

In the middle

In the middle of your story, your **characters** face a tricky problem. Here are some of the things that could go wrong in your animal story. Can you think of any more?

Ideas for the middle of the story

Dog gets lost or goes missing.

Dog behaves badly at home.

Dog's real owner turns up.

Dog gets injured.

Dog has to go to the vet.

One problem could be followed by another in your story.

Joe hid the dog in his bedroom. He called her "Scruffy". But Mum heard Scruffy barking. Luckily, Mum loved Scruffy, too.

"We can't keep her for ever," Mum said. "But she can stay until we find her a new home."

Joe hoped that Mum would change her mind.

 The middle of your story is also where the main action happens.

19

What happens next?

You might have several ideas for where your story will go next. How do you decide which is best? A **story map**, like the one below, can make it easier to work your ideas through.

Dog allowed to stay overnight.

1. Dog escapes in the night. Family never see dog again.

2. Dog chews Dad's shoes. Dad says dog must go.

You need to decide which direction your story will go in.

Next day, Joe rushed back from school to play with Scruffy. He threw a ball which Scruffy chased. Then Scruffy chased Joe around the garden. Scruffy was clever and Joe taught her to jump through a hoop. But Dad was cross with Scruffy. Scruffy had chewed a large hole in his best shoes.

Speaking parts

Use **dialogue** in your story to bring your **characters** to life. Dialogue means the words that people say. It can help to show your characters' personalities. It also breaks up large chunks of text.

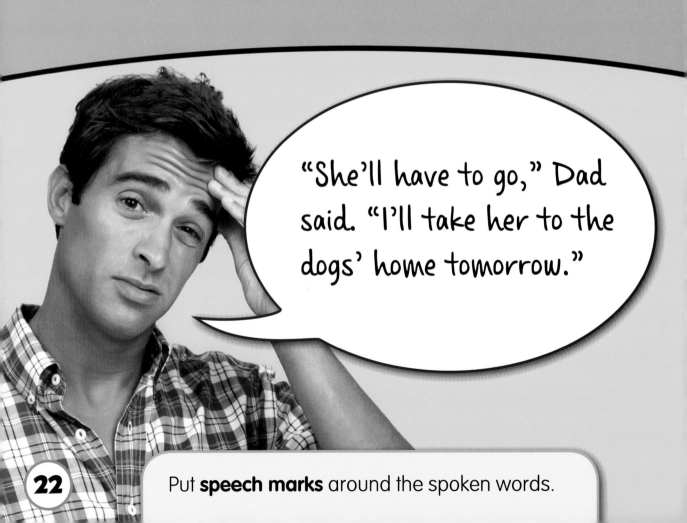

"She'll have to go," Dad said. "I'll take her to the dogs' home tomorrow."

Put **speech marks** around the spoken words.

"She'll have to go," Dad said. "I'll take her to the dogs' home tomorrow."

"But, Dad," said Joe. "She likes it here. We're her family."

"Sorry, Joe," said Dad. "I've made my mind up."

Sadly, Joe went up to his bedroom. Scruffy followed behind.

 Dialogue helps to bring your readers right into the story.

Points of view

The story in this book is written in the **third person**. It is as if the writer is watching the action. Try retelling the story from a different point of view. You could pretend that you are Joe or Scruffy.

Joe's dad didn't want me to stay. I was very sad and so was Joe.

These sentences are written from Scruffy's point of view.

In the night, Joe woke up suddenly. Scruffy was barking and scrabbling at the bedroom door.

"Ssshhh, Scruffy," said Joe. "You'll wake everyone up. And we're in enough trouble already."

But Scruffy kept barking. Joe opened the door and Scruffy ran into the kitchen. Joe saw water splashing. The tap was on and there was water all over the floor.

Try rewriting the whole story from Scruffy's point of view.

Happy ending

The ending of your story is where you tie up any loose ends. It is also where your **characters** solve their problems. Your ending can be happy or sad, or have a clever or surprising twist. Here are some ideas for endings for the story in this book.

Endings

- Joe's parents still send Scruffy away.
- Scruffy becomes famous.
- Joe's parents get Joe a cat instead.
- Scruffy is allowed to stay.

Which ending would you choose?

Mum and Dad came running in. Everyone helped clean up the mess.

"I don't want Scruffy to go," said Joe, helping to mop the floor.

"Don't worry, Joe," said Dad. "Scruffy's a clever dog. If she hadn't woken us up, we would have had a flood. She can stay. And I'll get myself some tougher shoes!"

"Hooray!" whooped Joe. "Woof! Woof!" barked Scruffy.

Use your ending to tell your readers what happens to your characters.
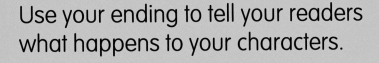

27

More top tips

1 Writing strong animal **characters** is just as important as writing strong human characters. Having a picture of the animal can help you decide what they are like.

2 Read lots of animal stories by other authors. This will help to spark off ideas and show you how other writers create good characters.

3 When you have finished writing, read and re-read your story. Rewrite any bits that you are not happy with.

4 Use **adjectives** and **adverbs** to make your writing more exciting. You can also include a mixture of long and short sentences to keep your writing interesting.

5 If you get stuck, try some automatic writing. Write down whatever comes into your head and see what happens.

6 If you set your story in a real place, such as a rainforest, make your description as accurate as possible. This will bring the **setting** to life.

Glossary

adjectives describing words that tell you about a noun (a noun is a naming word)

adverbs describing words that tell you about a verb (a verb is a doing word)

characters people in a piece of writing

dialogue words that characters say

fables stories that have a message to teach

fiction piece of writing that is about made-up places, events, and characters

plot what happens in a story

setting time and place in which a story is set

speech marks marks that show the words someone has spoken

story map diagram that helps you decide the next step of the plot

story mountain mountain-shaped diagram that helps you to plan out a story

third person using "he", "she", or "they"

timeline list of events in the order in which they happen

Find out more

Books

How to Write Stories, Celia Warren (QED Publishing, 2008)

Writing Stories, Anita Ganeri (Raintree Publishing, 2013)

Write Your Own Story Book, Louie Stowell and Jane Chisholm (Usborne Publishing, 2011)

Websites

www.bbc.co.uk/schools/ks2bitesize/english/writing

Learn how to improve your writing skills on this website.

www.readwritethink.org/files/resources/interactives/cube_creator/

The writing cubes on this website will help you to create your own stories.

Index